My Mother's Love♥

Pamela Tucker

Copyright © 2021 by Pamela Tucker

All rights reserved. This book or any portion thereof may not be reproduced or used in any manner whatsoever without the express written permission of the publisher except for the use of brief quotations in a book review.

All scriptures references are taken from the Holy Bible

Printed in the United States of America

First Printing, 2021

ISBN : 978-1-7350031-7-7

Email: Restartenterprise2017@gmail.com

CONTENTS

ACKNOWLEDGEMENTS 5

REMEMBERING MARY TUCKER 6

CHAPTER ONE 7

    THE -L- WORD 7

CHAPTER TWO 9

    TRAVELING DOWN MEMORY LANE 9

CHAPTER THREE 13

    FAMILY LOVE 13

CHAPTER FOUR 16

    MY MOM SERVED 16

CHAPTER FIVE 18

    MY MOM STORY OF THE MOON 18

CHAPTER SIX 20

    MY MOM SAID GIVE IT TO GOD 20

CHAPTER SEVEN 22

   MY MOM GIFT 22

CHAPTER EIGHT 25

   MY MOTHERS LOVE 25

CHAPTER NINE 29

   MY MOTHER POEMS 29

CHAPTER TEN 31

   MY MOTHER SAYINGS 31

CHAPTER ELEVEN 35

   LOVE 35

Acknowledgements

First I thank God for His grace, mercy and strength to complete this book without God none of this would have been possible.

To My Blessed Beautiful Family and Friends.

Thank you all for your prayers and support.

Thank you ALL for Loving my MOM

{Big Mama}

She Loved you All

REMEMBERING MARY TUCKER

Remembering Mary Tucker is so easy to do God blessed us with one of a kind and that was you. We remember you forever we talk about you still we tell of your words of encouragement so that others may be healed. You have never been forgotten and you never will we hold you close to our hearts and there you will stay until.

Remembering my mom {MARY TUCKER} and the Love she shared with our family, friends and others . I am sharing a few of her favorite sayings, poems, scriptures and stories.

CHAPTER ONE

THE -L- WORD

My friend invited me to a conference. I accepted the invitation. When I arrived I walked in, and the sign said the topic tonight is The L Word. Oh gosh, I immediately knew what they would be talking about night. Many people run from this word in relationship and in family in church or they use this word loosely. People use this word, but they don't demonstrate what the word really means. The Dictionary.com describes the L word like this { a feeling of warm personal attachment or deep affection, as for a parent, child, or friend.}

You should know by now the L word is LOVE

How does the bible describe the L word?

The Bible talks about these 4 words for Love.

There are four unique kinds of love that are revealed in the Bible. They are communicated through the Greek words: Eros, Storge, Philia and, Agape. Meaning Romantic love, Family love,

Brotherly love, and God's divine love. There are many more words to describe love, but today we're going to be talking about Storge Love, which is Family Love because we are going to be talking about a special family member and the love they shared. The speaker said we are going to be talking about

{ A Mother's Love}..

Even though the speaker was going to be talking about Storge { Family Love } I am thinking about all the different loves my mom showed to our family , friends, and others,

CHAPTER TWO

TRAVELING DOWN MEMORY LANE

Oh, wow a mother's Love, I'm here with all these people I got to get my emotions in check but this is so touching to me.

My mind is traveling back thinking about my mom. I have so many amazing memories about my mom. She was a special jewel to our family. I am so blessed to have had a mom like her.

A devoted mom is one who displays exceptional care and compassion towards her children, family and others around her.

She was also prayerful, loyal, adoring, and affectionate. Knowing that we had a loving, praying mother by our side helped us to get through so many difficult times in our family. Nothing else compares to having a praying, nurturing, loving mom.

My mom always said words of encouragement and wisdom to my siblings and me.

I remember my mom saying to me AJ you have to love God, yourself, and others. Then she would say we can't even love ourselves and others right if we don't love God. Then she said this scripture.

1 John 4:7-8 Dear friends, let us love one another, for love comes from God. Everyone who loves has been born of God and knows God. Whoever does not love does not know God, because God is love.

Someone once told me that God gave us an angel in disguise. My mom was exquisite, intelligent, full of wisdom and knowledge and loving. I don't think there's a woman like my mom anywhere she was so unique in every way she was slow to speak and quick to listen. She was a peacemaker, no matter what was going on she would say give it to God.

She was my shero. She was an amazing woman. She didn't have a prayer life, but she had a life of prayer meaning she lived a life of prayer. Everything else was incorporated in her life of prayer. She was always praying for her family, friends and others. People would call her to pray for them, I watched how she took time and prayed for them, but she also listened to them. It seems like she always had a prayer on the tip of her tongue.

I would listen to her and her best friend Evangelist Bell talking about the Love of God. They would quote the scriptures like

John **3:16** For God so loved the world that he gave his one and only Son, that whoever believes in him shall not perish but have eternal life.

The way they talked about God's Love was amazing to me as an eleven-year-old.

I would tell God thank you for loving me and sending His Son, that I may believe and be saved. They talked about so many scriptures about God's Love. Then Evangelist Bell said another scripture.

1Corintians 13

If I speak in the tongues of men or of angels, but do not have love, I am only a resounding gong or a clanging cymbal. If I have the gift of prophecy and can fathom all mysteries and all knowledge, and if I have a faith that can move mountains, but do not have love, I am nothing. If I give all I possess to the poor and give over my body to hardship that I may boast, but do not have love, I gain nothing. ...

Oh, they got so happy they started speaking in their heavenly language in between scriptures.

1John 4:18

There is no fear in love. But perfect love drives out fear, because fear has to do with punishment. The one who fears is not made perfect in love.

They were still going on about God's Love when I left the room. I was thinking my mom and evangelist Bell shared a special friendship as well. They could talk for hours and I do mean hours. I realize they had a great friendship with God and with each other. Both of them had some things incoming: they were God-fearing women. Both entrepreneurs; they were both married with families. They had balance, and they had so much Love for their families.

CHAPTER THREE

FAMILY LOVE

One day I watched my mom as she prepared to go before God in prayer, she would wrap her head up and had a certain way she would pray she was a loving wife to my dad for 49 years, a mother of four 1 boy and 3 girls. She was a proud grandmother of 17, a great grandmother of 19 and she loved them all and she would Pray for them all. My mom was an amazing woman of God, my mom worked as an entrepreneur for over 42 years, but she had balanced.

I remember when my sisters and I and our mom we went to the mountain we rode the train so many times that day, we had a picnic then my mom and my sisters got on the sky lift, now that was something because my mom did not do heights but we all got on and we laughed all the way up.

We had so much fun all that day.

One time we went to a park and the family came with my mom, grandchildren, her son-in-laws and daughter- in- law. We were celebrating my sister's birthday. We were playing old games like jack stones, old maid cards, water games and so much more. We laughed so much that day as well.

We were always having something at the house and everyone came over that Christmas aunties and uncles, friends , cousins ,grandchildren and family. We would have a spread out on the table and music going telling jokes, dancing, eating, playing games , passing out gifts and so much more. As some people say those were the good ole days.So much love

We were always coming together every sunday we would meet up at a restaurant or at the house. I remember a time we came to the house to break bread together and my dad liked to eat at whatever time you say dinner would be ready, but however, we like to wait for everyone that was coming so we were waiting for my brother to come.We had already told our dad a time and when that time hit I thought my dad was going to walk a path right from the sitting room to the kitchen. Yep those were the good ole days .

I remember my mom going to her grandchildren's graduation. She would always give them a card with money in it. She would be at whatever these grandbabies of hers was in plays talent shows spelling bee she was there.

I remember when my mom went to the movies or the picture show she called it. Like me put it like this we left before it was over. I am Laughing remembering that day. I have so many great memories.

CHAPTER FOUR

My Mom Served

I remember when dad and mom and the family would go to church my dad was a visiting preacher at this church and after service was over my mom would speak and leave in a little of a hurry. We would get home and my mom would start heating what she had cooked on Saturday for Sunday. She started frying chicken. MY mom used her best tablecloth for the dining room table. She made lemonade and sweet tea. We must be having some important people over to the house today thinking to myself. She had already made a cake and a pie. I was waiting to taste what I liked; I smell it. My mom opened the oven. Yum The cornbread is ready, she said yummy. My mom set the table oh what a spread. Collard greens, green beans with potatoes, homemade potato salad, corn on the cob, fried chicken, ham, Cornbread, rolls, sweet tea, lemonade, cake and pies, and all the trimmings. My mom used her dishes she keeps in her china cabinet. We use them sometimes, not just on special days she would every day is special. She goes and changes her clothes.

My mom comes out of the room and you could never tell she just prepared a dinner like this. She looks so beautiful to me not a hair out of place. She opens the front door and here comes my dad, the pastor and the preachers. My dad kisses my mom on the cheek as the pastor and preachers come in speaking to her. She tells them to have a seat in the dining room. They have a wet napkin and a dry napkin to wipe their hands. Now dinner is served. The conversation seems to be deep then the breakout of great laughter all while they were eating. They're finishing up; they go into the sitting room with coffee cake, pie or both. A little more small talk and a lot more laughter. So much Love. Now they are getting ready to leave they thanked my mom for extending her love and great hospitality.

CHAPTER FIVE

My Mom Story Of The Moon

I remember when I was a young girl we would go to church almost every other night during the week. I remember this night, especially since it was on a Tuesday night. We were on the way home from bible study and my mom saw the moon. It was so big, round and bright. I was in the backseat she was driving she said look Arianna look at the moon look how big it is and I was so fascinated with the wows of the moon it was so big and bright she said let me tell you this she said I see the Moon the Moon see me God bless the moon and God bless me. I was so mesmerized by what she had just said and looking at the moon. I said say it again listening to mom repeated again, Was a wow moment for me. The next thing I knew, she had passed the street where she was supposed to turn to go home. We ended up at a food place for a night snack .

I was still excited about what my mom had said. I was asking her all kinds of questions here. I am an 11-year-old thinking about what my mom had just told me about the moon.

Until this day Every time I see the moon I think of what my mom said to me that night over 40years ago, I was so fascinated with hearing it. I shared it with my children and grandbaby, friends .

CHAPTER SIX

My Mom Said Give It To God

I still remember it like it was yesterday. I remember so many wonderful things about my mom who was famous in the family for telling all of us if we had a problem TO GIVE IT TO GOD. We passed that saying to our families, friends and others.

My mom began saying that when I was a teenager. I never really paid any attention to it until, I had children of my own and life that I knew took a turn. I am grateful for an exceptional mom that did not just tell me how to be a wonderful mom to my own children, but she showed and told me how. She would say do what you can for your children and then give everything to God. Even what you desire to do for your children, give it to God. He knows what they need. He knows the desires of their heart. She said I never gave you everything you wanted, but you had what you needed and more because I gave it to God. Then she would tell me Arianna don't waste your words you will have to answer for them. I did not understand at first. I used to say what was on my mind until she gave me this scripture:

Matthew 12:36 Amplified Bible

But I tell you, on the day of judgment people will have to give an accounting for every careless *or* useless word they speak.

I still have to tell myself don't speak useless words let your words build others up in love .

CHAPTER SEVEN

My Mom Gift

I remember when I gave my mom teddy bears and balloons and stuffed animal's for unique occasions like {just because day}etc. I gave her and stuffed animal and this animal played music and the song title what does the fox say; oh wow I'm telling you my mom got up, and she started dancing and moving and boy we just cracked up laughing we laughed so hard that I was in tears because she just popped up and just started dancing and smiling had her arms up in the air dancing with the music and she was saying give it to God'. It's amazing remembering my mom Mary Tucker {Big Mama} . She was one of a kind. I absolutely miss my mom every single day. I think about the life that she lived and she would tell us her family and her friends and even people she didn't know, that may the life you live speak for you. Her life spoke volume even when her voice could not. I am so grateful to God for allowing me to experience getting to know and to get to touch someone so beautiful inside and out I had an amazing mom.

I Remember the month before my mom was transitioning she had stopped talking but I remember right before she stopped she looked at me in my eyes and she said remember Mary Tucker. Fighting back tears. I said to her, looking in her eyes how we can not remember Mary Tucker, my beautiful mom. My mom had such a special love for her family and others she was always there for us.

My mom had special words and scriptures she would say to her family together and to us individually.

I remember my mom saying that it's not about us, but it's about Jesus. I did not understand, but now I know what she was saying. It's about how Jesus demonstrated his love for us and about his teaching and preaching of the kingdom of heaven,

Matthew 4:17 From that time Jesus began to preach and say, "[a] Repent [change your inner self—your old way of thinking, regret past sins, live your life in a way that proves repentance; seek God's purpose for your life], for the kingdom of heaven is at hand."

She was such an amazing Woman.

CHAPTER EIGHT

MY MOTHERS LOVE

If I had to describe my mother's love with words I would use the alphabet.

Amazing- my mom was amazing in a lot of ways especially how she took care of her husband and her children, and how she loved her family, friends and others.

Brave- I watched my mom be brave when unexpected things happen in her life. You would have never known what she was going through.

Compassionate- My mom was compassionate with her family, friends and others.

Dependable- My Mom was dependable if she told you she was going to do something you could take it to the bank.

Empathetic- My mom had the ability to understand others emotions.

Faithful- My mom was faithful to God and her family until the end

Generous- My mom was always giving . She was happy to share her time, wisdom, knowledge , love , food, even her money and so much more with her family and others.

Helpful- My mom was always helping her family and her friends. She would travel the world to help others in need .

Inspiring - My mom made you feel like you could do anything as long as it was alright with God.

Jewel- My mom was priceless

Kindness- My mom was kind to everyone she met.

Loving-My mother Love can't be replace

Motivating- My Mom was always motivating family and friends and others to move forward to what God has planned for you.

Nurturing- My mom was a great nurture to me and my siblings

One Of A Kind- My mom is irreplaceable. There could never be a woman that could ever take her place.

Pulchritudinous- My mom was so Beautiful.

Quiet- My mom would speak volume even in her time of quietness.

Reliable- My mom was always there for the family. We could Rely on her.

Special- My mom had a special gift for helping and loving people.

Travel - My mom used to love to travel to see new things, new places and new faces.

Unique- My Mom had a unique way of choosing the right words to build people up with the word of God up no matter what they did.

Visionary- My mom was a seer

Wise- My mom was very wise in making decisions and she was not moved by circumstances nor people.

XOXOX- My mom loved to give hugs and kisses to her family.

Yes - My Mom use to tell us to give God a true yes

Zoom- My Mom use to drive fast zoom

CHAPTER NINE

My Mother Poems

★ A mother's love runs so deep my Mother Love was always sweet. My mother's love was so divine. I miss my mother all the time.Yet I share this poem with you knowing that it's a part of my heart and it's true

★ My Mother's love is deeper than the ocean goes, and it's as bright as the sunset that has ever been told.
Her love is unconditional; it has no strings attached.
She loved me, and that's a fact.
I can feel it in my heart til this day.
Her love is always with me, it never goes away.
Yet we're far apart; her love is always in my heart.

★ Thank you, mom, for having me. You could have stopped and changed your mind but, once again, your love shines and you pushed through all that God had for you which was me, your baby girl. I came in and settled your world. Thank you for every smile that fills the corners of my mind. Thank you for teaching me it's okay to bend and it's okay to break and that's in Prayer because God will build you back up. Thank you for giving me the roots to this life, Thank you for watering what God placed on the inside of me, but most of all, thank you for showing me that it's only GOD who causes the growth in me.

CHAPTER TEN

My Mother Sayings

- ★ Be A Help And Not A Hindrance

- ★ May the life I live speak for me

- ★ Your mouth has power, be careful what you speak.

- ★ Keep your faith up with the word of God.

- ★ Call on the name of Jesus Its power in that name.

- ★ All power belongs to God

- ★ Trust God

- ★ Devil Take your hand off of God's property

- ★ Don't think you are getting a way you are just getting by for now

- ★ Love God with all your heart

- ★ I Love you woo woo

My Mom 7 Day Prayer plan

Magnify Monday

Psalm 34:3

Oh, magnify the Lord with me,

And let us exalt His name together.

Testimony Tuesday

1 John 5:11 And this is the testimony: that God has given us eternal life, and this life is in His Son.

Worship Wednesday

Psalm 95:6 Oh come, let us worship and bow down;

Let us kneel before the Lord our Maker.

Thankful Thursday

Psalm 107:1

Oh, give thanks to the Lord, for *He is* good!

For His [a]mercy *endures* forever.

Freedom Friday

Galatians 5:1 It is for freedom that Christ has set us free. Stand firm, then, and do not let yourselves be burdened again by a yoke of slavery.

Sabbath Saturday

Hebrews 4:9 There remains, then, a Sabbath-rest for the people of God;

Salvation Sunday

Acts 4:12 Salvation is found in no one else, for there is no other name under heaven given to mankind by which we must be saved."

As you practice the 7 day a week prayer plan it keeps you thinking about the goodness of Jesus and the mercy and grace of God and the Holy Spirit

Everyday you have to pray.

CHAPTER ELEVEN

LOVE

Love is so important sometimes we don't show it like we should we all have room to do better. Jesus showed his love for humanity by dying on the cross , raisen up , and sitting on the right side of God interceding for you and I and all who believes in Him.

Would you die to fussing, arguing, complaining, murmuring would you die to hatred, killing, wrong thinking, manipulation, lies, etc.... and live a life of LOVE.

Show your Love to your family and friends and even the people you meet you never know you could entertain an angel unaware. Hebrews 13:2

John 15:12 My command is this: Love each other as I have loved you.

Remembering My Mom { Mary Tucker }

Always In My Heart

I LOVE YOU ☐

www.ingramcontent.com/pod-product-compliance
Lightning Source LLC
Chambersburg PA
CBHW051714090426
42736CB00013B/2696